GOD'S CALL UPON YOU!

GOD'S CALL UPON YOU!

Sharon Webb Jackson

Rev. date: 10/19/2021

To order additional copies of this book, contact:
Xlibris
844-714-8691
www.Xlibris.com
Orders@Xlibris.com
834058

CONTENTS

Prelude

God is calling us to be more like him. However, we live in a world that does not reflect his kingdom on this earth. There are so many people proclaiming to be Christians; however, our behavior and actions are not reflective of his love and presence. We make statements about being a Christian, but let someone upset you. As his chosen vessels, it is our responsibility to be a reflection of him each day. This book was inspired by the number of events that have occurred in my life. Each event had a different level of distress or despair, but the Spirit of God that resides within me did not allow the circumstances around me not to call on his great name. I will continue to call him "Aba, Father" as he is the great provider. I know that I am from another kingdom, living on the planet earth, and serving another king each and every day. Psalm 37 comes from David.

> Do not fret because of those who are evil
> or be envious of those who do wrong;
> ² for like the grass they will soon wither,
> like green plants they will soon die away.
>
> ³ Trust in the LORD and do good;
> dwell in the land and enjoy safe pasture.
> ⁴ Take delight in the LORD,
> and he will give you the desires of your heart.

^{5} Commit your way to the LORD;
trust in him and he will do this:
^{6} He will make your righteous reward shine like the dawn,
your vindication like the noonday sun.

^{7} Be still before the LORD
and wait patiently for him;
do not fret when people succeed in their ways,
when they carry out their wicked schemes.

^{8} Refrain from anger and turn from wrath;
do not fret—it leads only to evil.
^{9} For those who are evil will be destroyed,
but those who hope in the LORD will inherit the land.

Even those who are faithful and obedient in their relationship with Christ will sometimes face experiences that involve danger, fear, and despair. At times, the circumstances will exceed their natural ability to endure. When severe troubles occur in our lives we need not feel that God has abandoned us or has stopped loving us. Rather, we must remind ourselves that these things have happened to God's faithful people throughout history. God sometimes allows us to experience desperate times so that we might not rely on ourselves but on God. When we realize that Christ is with us and we look to him in faith, he will give us strength to endure and come through the situation victoriously (2 Corinthians 1:8-10).

Who's report do you believe

We need to unwrap your gifts and believe in his report

Human beings were created by God with a spirit, soul, and body (Genesis 1:27; 1 Thessalonians 5:23). It has been said that we are not bodies with souls; we are souls that have bodies. The body, the "outer man" is our physical housing through which we experience the world. Our souls are the personality centers of our beings from which our mind, will, and emotions operate. With our souls we choose either to listen to and obey the lusts of our flesh or the desires of the Holy Spirit (Galatians 5:16–17; Romans 8:9; Mark 14:38). The soul of a person is the courtroom where life decisions are made. He desires that we surrender those bodies as living sacrifices to Him (Romans 12:1–2). When we accept God's gift of salvation through Christ, our bodies become temples of the Holy Spirit (1 Corinthians 6:19–20; 3:16).

Many times you never acknowledge the good things that are happening on the inside of yourself. Your inner man is always competing with other aspects of your life. How often do you dream of a better tomorrow like a child? Children have a very unique creativity that dwells within them because of their hope. They allow themselves to explore and believe in a better tomorrow. They are forgivers. They do not hold any malicious feelings toward one another. Their interactions are honest and pure. We have the same hidden gems within us. They are God-given gems with our talents, skills, and abilities. God gives them to each of us to help us build up His church. The spiritual gifts in you are greater than any materialized gift you can give or receive from someone. Spiritual gifts are special; all of our talents, skills, and gifting come from him. He is the one who's knitted us together in the womb. He is also the one who enables us to be born again by the Spirit, Jesus Christ.

It does not matter where you are in life. God is with you. You gifts could be manifested here in the natural if you would only believe.

Think upon this revelation.

The first Adam is of the natural world, which is earth. We were made from the dust of the earth. Our spirit did not come alive until Jesus was born and died on the cross. He was sent here by God to do his will for us. The second Adam is the spirit. There are two forces occurring at the same time. Although the sprit is inside of you; you are fighting with your natural senses and overwhelming the spirit. You believe that your first thoughts are always correct, but that is not of god. God is love, kindness, and always abounding in the mercy of others. You choose to have this selfishness enter your heart and overtake your mind. There is a veil of darkness surrounding your thoughts and beliefs, but until you accept Jesus Christ as your lord and savior that veil is not removed. You need to make the decision and ask Jesus to come into your life and set you free. That is the second Adam, the spirit of God. You must believe that he can be manifested in your life to have you reconciled with him and make things right on your behalf. Jesus is the true vine and the connection to setting yourself free from the darkness of oppression which allows you to have true liberty. This freedom cannot occur until you agree. Your agreement will unlock the cares of this life and you will begin to have faith in our savior.

Genesis 2:7 speaks of the first man, Adam, becoming a living person. Adam was made from the dust of the ground and given the breath of life from God. Every human being since that time shares the same characteristics. However, the last Adam or the "second Adam"—that is, Christ—is a life-giving Spirit. Just as Adam was the first of the human race, so Christ is the first of those who will be raised from the dead to eternal life. Because Christ rose from the dead, He is "a life-giving spirit" who entered into a new form of existence. He is the source of the spiritual life that will result in believers' resurrection. Paul is here pointing out the difference between two kinds of bodies, i.e., the natural and the spiritual.

This revelation was not revealed until I began to step deep into the lord and here his promises to me. He revealed his power and glory to me as I became fully aware of whom I am in him. There is nothing that I need to do to have these promises. They are freely given to me because I believe and have faith in him that he is my lord and savior. He is everything to me. Spiritual gifts are special; God-given talents, skills and abilities; All of our talents, skills, and gifting come from God.

In the winter of 2018, I was attending my normal church service and during praise and worship I heard the lord say, you are going to go through the fire and I will bring you out. The fiery furnace would be hot however I would walk through it not being touched. I had no idea of the words that were being revealed to me because I never imaged that I would be having an experience of that kind. I was dealing with pressure at work. I had an employee that wasn't reliable. This employee made decisions that disrupted the lives of children and families. Children were displaced unnecessarily due to poor communication. My heart broke. I was addressing different issues day in and day out about this employee's inability to perform. I took information to people above me in hopes of things changing. There were more excuses on the employee's behalf. As time progress, the employee revealed the concerns that were preventing them from being productive and gave me my confirmation. I thought I was in the furnace at the time. I was not. Time had passed and the emotional roller coaster began to settle down.

During that time, I had to remind myself that I love God not because of what he can do for me but because of who he is. Loneliness despair hurt pains are all emotions you feel when you give your all and things are not working in your favor. I remembered that I was already free because God is within. He gave his all for us because he wanted to be a savior for you and me. The same spirit resting inside of you is the same spirit that rested in Jesus.

People of God, he was not only speaking but he was speaking directly to me about the chain of events that were going to occur in my life. I thought I had faith then and understood my relationship with the father but he took me deeper. I was going deeper and deeper in him. I could feel him wrapping his arms around me as I traveled this journey.

Psalm 31 is a prayer of David in distress, full of trust in God, and in Luke 23 the Son of David echoes the same prayer:

"In you, Lord, I have taken refuge;
let me never be put to shame;
deliver me in your righteousness.
Turn your ear to me,
come quickly to my rescue;
be my rock of refuge,
a strong fortress to save me.
Since you are my rock and my fortress,
for the sake of your name lead and guide me.
Keep me free from the trap that is set for me,
for you are my refuge.
Into your hands I commit my spirit;
deliver me, Lord, my faithful God"

I had to re-evaluate my level of commitment in him. I began to slow myself down and remind myself of that covenant we made together. A covenant is a promise between two or more parties to perform certain actions. A covenant is very similar to a promise.

God made several covenants. Here are two examples,

God made a covenant with Noah that He would never again destroy the world by a flood, and He also gave some basic principles for humanity to live by (Genesis 8:20—9:17). Although humanity soon descended into rampant disobedience once again, the promise not to destroy the earth by another flood was unconditional.

God made a covenant with Abraham in which He promised, "I will make you into a great nation, and I will bless you; I will make your name great, and you will be a blessing. I will bless those who bless you, and whoever curses you I will curse, and all peoples on earth will be blessed through you" (Genesis 12:1–3).

The concept of covenant has been lost in modern society. Promises are broken when new circumstances arise. Marriage is supposed to be a covenant between a man and a woman for life, but divorce is commonplace today. Regardless of how unfaithful people may be, God will never be unfaithful to His covenant promises.

A promise is something that you prioritize in your life in order for things to be established. We can't just hope and pray for things to come to past. We need a level of commitment to God, to others and to ourselves. Commitment exercises your accountability level. Promises are broken when new circumstances arise. People don't want to be accountable for their actions. Often times they make escape routes for their bad behavior but God is watching your every move. You can't hide from him. He see.. He knows and he is watching your every move.

We need to stop wasting time avoiding what he has called you to do. Let's take a look at Hagar. Hagar was Sarah's servant. God promised Abraham that an heir from his own body would have innumerable descendants. Abraham believed in the Lord, and it was credited to him as righteousness (Genesis 15:6). While Abraham believed in God that He could and would keep His word, Abraham had no idea how God would accomplish that. His wife Sarah figured out a way for God to keep His promise. Her idea was that Abraham could have a child through Hagar, Sarah's servant (Genesis 16:1–2). Hagar conceived quickly, and Sarah became jealous (Genesis 16:4). Sarah treated Hagar badly—so badly, in fact, that Hagar even while pregnant fled into the wilderness to escape the mistreatment (Genesis 16:6–7).

The angel of the Lord appeared to Hagar, and, after encouraging her to return to Sarah, He promises Hagar that He would multiply and bless her descendants through the child she would bear (Genesis 16:10–12). Because He saw her in a time of distress when she was hiding and journeying in the wilderness, Hagar acknowledged Him as *El Roi*, that is, "the God of Seeing," or "the God Who Sees"

Begin to commit to his will and his way. You need to stop pretending as if you are moving in the right way because your level of commitment is shaky. You are not committed. You are falsifying things because you don't want anyone to hold you accountable. Stop pretending you pretender. Be willing to take a stand and do the things he wants you to do. Being committed shows accountability and makes things happen.

Commitment requires your undivided attention and focus. The lord is looking for individuals that will not compromise he's looking for people that are committed. Your intentions are always good but your actions provide evidence as to who you are. He will use you in his plan if you're committed to his cause and not your own. We often want things in our own time but take a look around and experience the talents he's placed within you. I remember working on a job and the people did not treat me fairly. I would come up with ideas and strategies on how to work more effectively and efficiently. Although the ideas were good; I never received the proper credit. However, I stayed committed to that job. I was looking for commitment in the natural but God reminded me that I needed to work as if it was unto him. He is in control of all things. Each day, I do my best because God expects excellence from me.

Questions for Study

1. What are your special talents or gifts? Are you using them? Is God pleased with you?

_____
_____
_____
_____
_____

2. Do you have anything to offer someone? If so, what?

_____
_____
_____
_____
_____

3. Do you believe the talents or gifts are from the Lord, Jesus Christ?

_____
_____
_____
_____
_____

Life Application

Spiritual gifts are special, God given talents, skills and abilities that are given to each of us to help build his church.

Faith Response

Proverbs 18:16, A gift opens the way for the giver and ushers him into the presence of the great

Let the Lord use you to be a blessing for someone else

The testing of your faith

Have you ever considered your level of faith? Do you think you have the faith to move a mountain? Can you stand in the gap for others? Are you willing to be embarrassed or ashamed for God? Have you ever considered what others will say about you as you wait upon the Lord to do his work? God is calling us to show ourselves mighty for him. Here I am writing in the midst of a storm that has me waiting, searching, praying, unsettled, and worrying as I dream of my deliverance out of this dark place. I have never been in such despair. However, God knew I would be right here having this experience and turning my heart toward him once again because I don't know any other way. He is the only one I can count on to help me overcome any obstacle that has been placed in my way and I come to you saying......people of God, turn your hearts toward him.

It's the only way.

I would like to share my journey with you about how God moves in my life. He has never left me alone. I have had so many twists and turns in my life, but he keeps bringing me out because I keep my focus him. Life is funny. There have been times my faith is low but the individuals that are close to me whether it's a family member or friend; they always lead me back to my father, Jesus Christ. I love that people know, who

I am and who's I am in my time of trouble without hesitation because they know my heart. It's not a question in their sight.

When I was a child I dreamed about God giving me a business to help others. I would be on my mother's bed talking about this plan for hours and hours. I would state that people would come to me for me to provide them with a service. My desire has always been about giving of myself to others. I was passionate about beginning my program of helping others. I believed my education was the key I needed to propel me into my purpose but all along I have been living it out. Each day, I help someone besides myself. Whether, it's an encouraging word, gesture, smile, or action. I am living out this desire. I am a daughter, a sister, a wife, a mother, a friend, a supervisor, and a teacher. I have been walking in this position for several years helping and encouraging others along the way. All along, God has been showing me my purpose. My purpose is to walk out the things he's placed inside of me each day; and I am getting better and better.

At the onset of my career, I was employed at the hospital working in the pediatric department with children and families. I believed this was the best opportunity to obtain experience and connections but it was a God ordained experience. You may say; how was God involved in a hospital clinic. I am glad you've asked.

In the clinic, my supervisor was not only one of the leaders in the social work department, but she was also a professor at a local university within the city. She was well known within the community. I had a great deal of respect for her and her professional knowledge. I believed that she was going to teach me so much. Her favorite phrase was "I come with a wealth of knowledge", which I utter today. I believed that she was very knowledgeable and would give me access to great opportunities' as we all do. During my experience, she did not give me the insight I was expecting her to pass along because she carried a weight herself. I had placed her higher than God. She lacked her own confidence in herself to stand upright in the gifts she carried. When I was working with her,

I became pregnant and at the time I was not married. She immediately told me that I needed to place a ring on my finger because it was disrespectful for me to continue to work in this environment; unwed and pregnant. She was more concern about the doctor's thoughts or actions toward me. I felt guilt and shame for having another child without being married. I found myself feeling embarrassed and hopeless. I sat in the seat of her criticism. I thought, is this my employer or my mother? The lines were so blurry. How dare she? Who does she think she is? It was such an unexpected conversation for an employer to have with an employee. She stated "how can you counsel someone else about utilizing birth control and you didn't; what will the doctors say". She wanted to please the people instead of helping the people. At that moment, I was having the same experience as some of the patients. I realized I carried a passion for helping others and my desire to grow was not being flourished because she considered me and the patients as less. I could feel their pain of being a single mother wanting something different but sitting in their experience.

There was one valuable lesson in that experience; she helped me to lean on God. I had always attended church regularly with my family and knowing about getting help from the Lord. I remember speaking with one of my co-workers and pouring my heart out to her. She could not console me but she knew who could. I never knew this co-worker's mother was a minister. We would spend a lot of time with one another and she never told me but there was something very special about our relationship. On that day, she called her mother as I sat in my office wearing a red dress with a red and white striped shirt. Her mother read the sinners' prayer to me and I accepted Jesus into my life and I never looked back. Her mother ministered to me not only in her words, but she encouraged me along the way. She sent me my first Bible that I still have till this day. I knew about God, but I didn't know him like that. I was excited about this new found relationship that was bubbling on the inside of me. I shared the news with my family and no one believed me but I didn't' stop. The lords' warm embrace was with me.

Several weeks after giving my life to Christ, I married my husband. Although, I had given birth to one child and had one on the way, God was still with me and letting me know that my sins were forgiven. I was extremely anxious about getting married to my husband because his family was all church going people and I thought I was not good enough for him. "Am I holy enough for them all". However, my husband accepted me with all my doubts. As I look back, I realize that we all fall short. The defining moment for me was everyone sins. My sin just produced children. We all fall short from God's glory and he continues to care for us.

I believe God placed me in that environment to see me reconnect with him. I want you to never miss his blessings and guidance. According to (Ephesians 2:10), For we are God's handiwork, created in Christ Jesus to do good works, which God prepared in advance for us to do.

I worked extremely hard for that supervisor in every capacity. I decided to leave that place and move in another direction to learn more about the helping profession. Shortly after I departed my position, she was moved around because the work was not moving the same. I received a telephone call from someone and they asked my "how did you do this daily?" The only explanation I could provide was with God's help. He was walking along side me; and the person that took my position was a minister. The favor of God was on my life to work with the children and families. At that moment, I didn't question his call for my life.

I began working within another agency that not only cared about the children, but also the families. I learned how to advocate for the children, biological parents, foster parents, and work well with providers. The leadership team respected their employees and growth happened. I was able to bring different ideas and creativity to the team. The relationships between children and families were being built. I had the opportunity to teach people how to communicate with one another and show them how to have love for one another, which made relationships happy and healthy. I loved the insight that I was acquiring in that experience, but things changed. I had a relative say to me "why are you working so hard for pennies; you should get paid for working". The thought of money clouded my mind and judgment. I stepped out and made the transition of my life. I didn't take the opportunity to pray and ask the father if this was "what" he wanted for my life. I did exactly what people in the world do. I believe that this transition was in my best interest for me as well as my family. I was moved by the world's standards of having more money in my pocket. However, I continue to pay for that decision as I have endured a lot of heart ache and pain.

I have had some hard lesson but with the help of the Lord Jesus Christ; I have managed to overcome some many obstacles. The hurt, pain, and disappointment from family, friends, co-workers, and other individuals was a struggle. God kept me and keeps showing me my worth or sending people along my path to encourage me to keep going and leaning on him. I love a word from one co-worker and I often go back to it to remind myself of God's love towards me, he would say, "you are so graceful like a dove above the water, but I'm sure underneath the water, you are flapping away". He was speaking truth in that moment. My outward appearance never reflects the level of battles that are occurring in my life.

There were many times; when I walked in disbelief of my relationship with God or hearing his words. I received a word from the lord through a prophet, "he said, delight in what some cannot see, the beauty of the lord is in thee, so stand alert and stand high; you saint of the most high". I often pull that word out to remind myself of God's word because people have thought otherwise. I spent so much time on the thoughts of others and never realizing what God thinks about me. I don't talk much about what God has revealed to me, but I write his words down all the time. He speaks to me; he reveals things to me in dreams; he sends people to me to remind me of my purpose here on the earth. He allows me to use my gifts when necessary to encourage others along their journey. I know what he has called me to do. It's not something coming from the outside in, but something awaking on the inside, which impacts the things around me. My faith has encouraged others to believe in his word for themselves. I walk upright believing in his word each and every day. I have trusted the lord in every situation. Even when others doubt my motives or actions, I believe that God will reveal, who I am. I have learned to live for an audience of one. I go into my secret place and spend time with the lord; praying, worshipping; and thanking him for every good work he has done for us. He gives us new mercies each day. Every day, I walk in the anointing he placed on my life. I am committed to my anointing.

Have you ever had the experience of someone questioning your faith or trying to discredit your belief in the lord?

There I was thrown into a fire with people that looked like me, stated they love God like me, but their behavior indicated something totally different. The evilness was evident that they didn't know the father because their behavior did not reflect his love. Each day, I would go into my office and pray for God to give me strength. I didn't ask for his strength sometimes, but continually because I was at war. This was not a physical war but a spiritual battle that I knew I could not fight alone. I reminded myself about the kingdom that I was a part of. The reminders were posted all around me. My favorite saying is "my connection is divine". You may ask how you know the person was evil. The lord allowed me to see the evilness up front and in person.

It was a fall day. I was packing up to leave work for the day. Earlier that day, a youth was in crisis and needed a place to stay. A meeting was held and we arranged a plan for the youth's placement in hopes of all things going well. Prior to me leaving, she asked me about the results of the meeting as I was present. I assumed she was fine with the plan but the other supervisor never consulted her about the plan. The manger became angry with the team because the decision was made and she did not agree. She thanked me for my participation and

*her postured turned to the other supervisor and worker.
I remember her mouth twisting; she began yelling and
screaming at them. I saw a mask come over her like I've
never seen in my life. It was frightening. I asked her
to calm down and breathe because I felt like she was
going to have a medical crisis due to her response. At
that moment, the clinical director had to get involved to
help facilitate and deescalate the conversation. My heart
was beating fast and I didn't know if I should leave the
people or stay. After that experience, the supervisor and
worker never had the freedom to advocate for another
youth.*

This was the first illustration of how she inflicted the harm towards the staff. I was not aware of the behavior as I was new to the environment. The next day, I was informed that was normal behavior for her but since I was new, I never witnessed it. After that experience, she began to reveal herself. I never had the courage to advocate for myself but God's boldness got a hold of me. When I saw others walking in despair and hurting, I knew someone had to say something. I realized that was me. The pressure was overwhelming and I was afraid but I called my pray partners and said pray for me I'm going into battle. I knew I could not face this battle alone. The battle was confronting the evilness in its face. I had to strategize my thoughts, my feelings, and my actions. It wasn't my strategy it was God's. He prepared me for the battle. At that moment I realized I was fighting against spirits. A spirit that believed they control everything but only our Lord and Savior has full control of things. Although the prayers occurred their words also reminded me that as a believer in Jesus Christ the victory already occurred over 2000 years ago and he gave me the keys needed to my destiny. At that moment I looked in the mirror and said I am a child of God. I became his child when I accepted him into my life 20 years ago. The day I gave my life to him was the most rewarding experience. At that moment, I felt alone and I was hurting. I needed someone to tell me I was going to be okay and he did. Jesus was a present comforter and he keeps providing me with comfort each and every day. Whenever I'm in despair, he reminds me of that embrace. We can't always see him at each moment but there is an assurance of faith that God is by your side. You must always trust and believe in him.

As I set out to place my confidence in him; I went home and began to search the character of a person that wanted to inflict hurt and pain on someone to be better equip myself in this world system. I stated to the lord I need your wisdom and a strategy. I would go to the scriptures to get direction and instruction. I needed to make sense out of that experience because I was told she believed God like me. I was walking in disbelief because I could not see God's love or presence radiating in her. She would think of ways to frustrate someone peace. All I could see was wickedness. I looked at several bible stories about people who plotted to do harm to others. For example, I found King Herod to be a person that wanted to inflict harm on our lord and savior, Jesus Christ. According to Matthew 2:16, after King Herod discovered that the Christ was to be born in Bethlehem, "he sent and killed all the male children in Bethlehem and in that entire region who were two years old or under. He wanted to inflict harm on all the innocent individuals that weren't doing any harm to anyone. This decree impacted not only the individuals inflicted but others around them. Families were suffering because of his fear of his position. Individuals will do anything to hurt others to gain control. Control is the power to influence or direct people's behavior or the course of events. Herod wanted the wise men to tell him about the messiah but they did not obey his decree. Each day, I walk in the obedience of the lord because the inflection that she requires me to do does not line up with the word of the lord.

Whenever someone thinks of ways to create or frustrate someone peace, it's evil. Jesus would never think of ways or look for ways to create harm or hurt to others. Yet he does place us in trials or tribulation, but to show us who he is in the storm. I could see the people hurting as well as myself.

Take another evil one, Jezebel. She was a heathen princess who married Ahab, king of Northern Israel [plot twist: he turned out to be just as evil], and was heavily involved in idolatry and wicked schemes. After King Ahab married Jezebel, it was as if she were king because she so influenced King Ahab that she led the nation further and further away from God and deeper and deeper into pagan worship. He cared for over 800 false prophets and killed many of the true prophets, and even sought to kill Elijah. This wicked woman even arranged for the murder of a vineyard owner named Naboth when her husband could not take control of the land by himself (1 Kings 21).

People make a choice not to be kind. There is no force preventing you from doing the right thing you choose to be evil.

The lord Jesus Christ allows us to show love and kindness to those who have done wrong to us. He allows your heart to be overcome with his grace and mercy for forgiveness. It's his unselfish way of showing his glory here on the earth. The love of the father is so rich and rewarding. To understand his love you need to set aside your beliefs and hold on to his plan and purpose. There are no conditions for his love. His love crosses all cultures, race, ethnicity, and systems.

We have been told to group people together based upon a certain status. Take the limits off of God and love with a pure heart because he first loved you. Be free and love again.

I was tested on every side to do what she wanted even if it was wrong. I set up a clear boundary as to who I was going to serve. I did not serve the pagan atmosphere. I made a clear decision to service Christ. I would not allow her to compromise my relationship with the father.

There is no good thing the lord will withhold from us. We are instructed to follow his ways here in the earth and mimic him. We walk in the way of the unrighteousness when we place ourselves in submission to things of this world. The lord doesn't need you battling for things. God will order your steps if you are moving in the direction he has called you into. People of God, you should not be trying to make things happen. He will make them happen in time. God is calling you higher to his will and way. We need to humble ourselves to his plan and purpose. We need to seek him and only him.

Questions for Study

1. How has God tested you?

   _____

   _____

   _____

   _____

   _____

2. What scriptures did you stand on during your test?

   _____

   _____

   _____

   _____

   _____

3. Were you committed to serving God and making the changes?

   _____

   _____

   _____

   _____

   _____

Life Application

Remember to stand strong in any test or trial with the Lord Jesus Christ in the midst of the problem or situation

Faith Response

1 Kings 10:1, When the queen of Sheba heard about the fame of Solomon and his relation to the name of the Lord, she came to test him with hard questions

Be Strong in the Lord and in the power of his might

Standing in God's peace

There is no need to question who you are or whose you are because you are a child of the king. The king has all power and authority in his hands. There is no one or nothing that doesn't pass through him. He knows the circumstances you are facing at this very moment. He understands your doubts or disbelief. He has experienced them himself in gethsematy. Jesus was in the midst of questioning his next steps as he walked out his journey just like us. We often question whether or not the decision that is being made is the best decision but God. Let's take a look at this story.

The story of the Garden of Gethsemane can be found in Matthew 26:36-56, Mark 14:32-52, Luke 22:39-53, and John 18. After the Last Supper in the Upper Room, after Judas left to notify the chief priests that Jesus would be vulnerable, Jesus led His remaining disciples to the Garden of Gethsemane. The garden, possibly an olive grove ("gethsemane" means "oil press"), sat on the side of the Mount of Olives. John 18:1 describes the area as "over the ravine of the Kidron."

Once Jesus and the disciples arrived, Jesus drew away Peter, James, and John—His core three followers. He asked them to stay with Him. "My soul is deeply grieved, to the point of death; remain here and keep watch with Me" (Matthew 26:38). He then went a little farther, fell to His face, and, in agony, asked God to find another way. His sweat fell like drops of blood; God sent an angel to comfort Him. We cannot know the depths of Jesus' sorrow at this time. While Jesus wept in anguish, Peter, James, and John fell asleep.

Jesus returned to the three and woke them up. "So, you men could not keep watch with Me for one hour? Keep watching and praying, that you may not enter into temptation; the spirit is willing, but the flesh is weak" (Matthew 26:40-41). Again He prayed, humbly and actively submitting to the will of God. But filled with good food and wearied from an emotional night, the disciples fell asleep again.

Jesus rose. When He found them sleeping again, He let them be. He reiterated His distress of what He must do, as well as His willingness. Then He returned to His disciples and woke them, saying, "Arise, let us be going; behold, the one who betrays Me is at hand!" (Matthew 26:46).

As Jesus spoke, Judas arrived, followed by a large number of men with swords, lanterns, and clubs—a Roman cohort (of 300-600 men) as well as officers from the chief priests and Pharisees. Judas called to Him—calling Him "Rabbi," or teacher—and kissed Him, a traditional greeting at the time. In case they didn't get the picture, Jesus asked the soldiers who they were looking for. When they said "Jesus the Nazarene," Jesus responded, "I am He."

Jesus submitted to the mob as He began His fulfillment of His role of Messiah, the Anointed One.

He was wondering his next move or steps that needed to be taken but the father revealed unto him that he needed to walk in his purpose just like you and I. We cannot wallow in this disbelief of thinking our king is not in control. He has the legal authority to be. We asked for him to come in and do the necessary changes in our life to make us whole. He knocked and we allowed him in. So why do we question his will and way. Do you not see him at work? Do you not believe his power? Stop. He loved you and he continues to show you his love. God has you in his hands.

There is nothing great about me but my ability to follow my lord and savior. Jesus guides me in my every decision. He helps me in my weaknesses. His strength is greater than anything I could ever desire.

I remember God saying "we are one of his generals here in the earth if we accept Jesus Christ". Acceptance of Jesus Christ, places us under a new covenant. We are now entering into a new family system with different views and values. Value is a person's principles or standards of behavior; one's judgment of what is important in life. The only way to the father is by his son, Jesus Christ. We can only believe that report. Jesus died for all of our sins not some but all; we need to let him in to break down the barriers in our life. These barriers are the systems that are set up that are not like his. Each of us has different systems we follow that are not like God because they bring us comfort and joy or your parents did it. What does he say about the matter? God is a God of order. Jesus is our example only if we yield to his spirit. I remember riding on a train and the conductor asked me a question. At that moment, I was having an experience. My mind was telling me to say something rude and hurtful but what came out of my mouth was very different than what was going on in my head. That was my first real experience of knowing there are two different forces occurring on the inside of us. That rude nasty cold nature is not of God. That matter of fact attitude, tell it like it is….that's not him. He is loving, kind, gentle, and easy with everyone. We cannot go around saying and doing anything that comes to mind. Stop! Stop making you feel good. Stop hurting others by your malicious tactics. Church folk keep people stuck because we think we're telling the truth. Whose truth are you really telling? I have walked with God long enough that your behaviors and actions are examples of his truth. How you treat yourself and others show us who you really are. You need to be proactive by having his spirit of truth. Jesus see's good in everyone. Yes, we have faults. Yes we have made mistakes. Yes, we all sin. The scripture is clear that we are born into this sinful world, but he gives us the power of choice. Loving the things of this world is not of him. Each day, I pray for God to give me balance because he is a God of order. There is divine order in everything for him. He has a strategy to overcome this world. We don't' know his strategy until we spend time with him yielding to his spirit; talking with him, walking with him, living like him. He wants to teach us things. The glory that god has for us is magnificent. We need to begin to pick up our cross and live for that audience of one by any means necessary. You need to begin to speak these words......I will follow you lord and you alone lord. You are my god. Jesus is my example. He was bruised for my iniquities that chastisement is upon his shoulders. Jesus has already done so many great things for me here on earth. As I walk out what he asks me to do, I step deeper and deeper with him. In the past, I would wonder about my differences, but being set apart for his purposes stops me from questioning that any longer. I am not living for people. I am living for him. He is my sole example. There is no one like you lord.

It's interesting about this assurance of faith that I have. My faith is built on nothing but my wall of remembrance. Jesus has done so many things in my life. When any situation is bigger than me; he steps right in and helps in his timing; just because I am settled in his kingdom. Some people believe, it's not easy to be a part of a kingdom that requires you to be loving, kind, nice, and of good character. It takes discipline to stand in his light. The discipline is not following simple steps but the discipline to check in with him each and every second, minute, and hour. He is always there to give you the true direction you need to follow him but you need to stop and listen. I know there is someone who sits high and looks low at someone as small as me. I have experienced him interceding on my behalf. He cares about your every need. There is nothing he's not concerned about. He cares for every corner of our life. It took time for me to get to this place as I continue to walk out my journey on the earth.

The lord is looking for a people that are bold and willing to take a stand for what is right in the eyes of the lord. We should not be seeking things that do not represent him in the earth. He is the example will need to live up too. The father wants us to pattern our lives after him. He is the only one who sits above all things and makes them right. He knows the end before the beginning. I love that he takes care of me at all times. I don't know the plans he has for me, but I know he has me in his hands.

As a Christians, we need words of encouragement to lift one another out of our stuck positions. We need to challenge each other to take risk and step out on the things he has asked us to do.

So often people look at the outer things to determine where you should go and be but God is internal. He is always measuring your heart and motives. He looks at your actions. Your heart dictates your thoughts and actions. It informs you in the way you should go. Not leaning on your own understanding or direction but bringing forth clarity in life circumstances. In all things let your heart lead you as it's the center piece of your mind, will, and emotions.

Ask yourselves a few questions:

Am I being completely honest with myself?

What story do I want to tell later down the road (life events, school, college)?

Which decision can I make that's the most honoring to God?

Is there a tension that I need to give my attention too (moral)?

Timing is everything. A decision needs to be made to be a better you. You need to strive to be the same person in front of the crowd as you are behind the scenes; when the pressure is on. Be very careful not to conform. You see, character isn't who we say we are. It's who we actually are. You can fake. Learn to value the process of building your character. Character and Integrity are keys to building you. You need to get back in focus. Every time you are doing something for God it's not going to be easy.

Blessed is the man who trusts in the Lord, whose trust is the Lord. He is like a tree planted by water, that sends out its roots by the stream, and does not fear when heat comes, for its leaves remain green, and is not anxious in the year of drought, for it does not cease to bear fruit *(Jeremiah 17:7-8).*

Ways to Trust in the Lord with All Your Heart:

Proverbs 3:5 Trust in the LORD with all your heart and lean not on your own understanding (Don't depend on you)

Proverbs 3:6 in all your ways submit to him, and he will make your paths straight. (Cry out to God)

Proverbs 3:7 Do not be wise in your own eyes; fear the LORD and shun evil. (Run from evil)

Proverbs 3:9-10 Honor the LORD with your wealth, with the first fruits of all your crops; [10]then your barns will be filled to overflowing, and your vats will brim over with new wine (Put God First in Your Life)

Jeremiah 17:9 The heart is deceitful above all things and beyond cure. Who can understand it? (Check yourself by God's word)

John 14:16 And I will ask the Father, and he will give you another advocate to help you and be with you forever- (Listen to the Holy Spirit)

Proverbs 3:12 because the LORD disciplines those he loves, as a father the son he delights in. (Rest in God's Love)

Always be obedient to God. Do what is right in honoring God and make your decisions be reflective of God. Gethsemanty means oil-press, which is especially memorable for us as being the scene of his misery and torture. Jesus was in suffering to make the right decision but with prayer he did it.

Questions for Study

1. Do your thoughts and actions mirror him?

_____

_____

_____

_____

_____

2. Have you been taking examples from your new blood line?

_____

_____

_____

_____

_____

3. Are you walking in his assurance?

_____

_____

_____

_____

_____

Life Application

The lord is looking for a people that are bold and willing to take a stand for what is right in the eyes of the lord. Faith sincerely believes in God, entrusting one's life to his care, relying on him for help, strength, and trusting in his goodness.

Faith Response

Hebrews, 10:22, Let us draw near to God with a sincere heart in full assurance of faith, having our hearts sprinkled to cleanse us from a guilty conscience and having our bodies washed with pure water.

Are you Christ like?

Walking in his divine glory

The lord is showing us he is still on the throne. There is nothing that he is not a part of. During different seasons of life, he warns us to turn our hearts towards him. We are taught to rely on His great power to get us through trials such as a job loss, a sticky divorce, bankruptcy, hateful persecutions, a debilitating illness, or the loss of a loved one. Learning to rely on the power of God is part of living the Christian life. He is in control of all things and his glory reigns on the just as well as the unjust. As believers that have accepted Jesus Christ, his spirit dwells on the inside of us. We have an access to his goods; there are others that do not have access to his power. Although, he wants everyone to be saved; he also wants us to walk in the power and glory that has been placed upon us. We are the living examples. We are no longer slaves to sin

but we are reconciled to God. He is our father. We are both joint heirs (Galatians 3:29) and friends (John 15:15) of Christ. And this relationship is even stronger than those we have with our earthly families (Matthew 10:35–37). Instead of fearing God as judge, we have the great privilege of coming to Him as our Father. We can approach Him with confidence and ask of Him what we need (Hebrews 4:16). We can ask for His guidance and wisdom (James 1:5) and know that nothing will take us from Him (Romans 8:38–39). We can also rest in His authority and respond to Him with trusting obedience, knowing that obedience is a key part of remaining close to Him (John 14:23).

His requirements are not a lot. There are so many more requirements to follow living like the world. You are forced with the cares of this life and the people who dwell around you. Jesus was not worried about this life. He was focused on heavenly things. His spirit was filled with righteousness. The righteousness that God wants to see in the earth; so stop procrastinating and get moving and allow God to use you and bring things through you here in the earth. He is calling all of us back to him and the beginning stages are in prayer. Prayer is a vital part of relying on the power of God, as we pray, "Thy will be done" (Luke 11:2, KJV). Jesus said, "Ask, and it will be given to you; seek, and you will find; knock, and it will be opened to you. For everyone who asks receives, and he who seeks finds, and to him who knocks it will be opened" (Matthew 7:7–8). He not looking for some of us but he wants all parts of us to be made whole. He can heal our every wound if we allow him in. The beauty is once he fixes it; there is no need in looking back. It's all cleaned up and cleared out. There is no need to address it, patch it, or continue to nurse it because it's completely gone. He's wiped it all away. That is a part of his love and I thank him for loving me.

A friend once said to me "you must believe to receive". Believing in his power gives you strength. It is the supernatural strength to equip you to be on fire.

I have found that fear slows down my progress and power. Fear will let in different distractions and make you lose hope as well as increase anxiety.

Peoples' apprehension of you can block your success due to their inability to support you or be happy about your God given destiny/ talents; success happens over time and your focus needs to be linear. The vision should be clear to you for your achievements to occur. God is the only individual that needs to give it the stamp of approval. If it's a yes to him it doesn't matter if no one else sees the vision. Get moving on what God has caused you to do.

God often reminds me that there is nothing that occurs outside of his midst. He gives us the opportunity to seek him over and over again but we keep walking without him. Lord I thank you for allowing me to keep you at the forefront of my life. This lifestyle of serving him cannot be forfeited for anything. He is all we need during each season of life.

This glory walk with him is awesome I couldn't have asked for anything else. His peace is surrounding me day by day hour by hour minute by minute. Every second I'm reminded of his grace and mercy. His protection has been magnificent. This protection the Lord gives extends beyond yourself. I see my covenant with the Lord has extended to my children and with this leap of faith it will extend to my grandchildren. We are the seed planters and his word waters each seed. I believe that he has allowed me to plant not only within my family but outside of my inner circle. That is the life he has called each of us to do. At times, I do not see it right away but the behavioral changes I see in individuals reassures me that my relationship with Christ has had an impact on someone besides myself. I no longer worry or not if the words I say, are good because he is my mouth piece. They are coming directly from the center piece of my life which is my heart and anyone that has an ear to hear knows that in the middle of heart is "ear". I can't describe it in any other way; walking in his footsteps gives me such joy to know that a savior has gone before me. It's not just anyone but the one true Man, Jesus Christ. Jesus has created this lifestyle of service for us to model. The model is without any spots or wrinkles but he keeps giving us another chance to make it right. Why struggle? His ways has so many more benefits than we could ever obtain on our own. Jesus' benefits are a yes and amen. He has paid it all. This was his sacrifice to the world. He laid it all down for you and me. What more could we ask for?

God has been so good to us. He deserves everything. There is nothing that doesn't belong to him. He is worthy to have it all. My people give it all to him. He is so worthy. You are worthy lord.

His glory is revealed to others when you don't speak your testimony but you are living your testimony. God will have us walk out things where people have a limited amount of information and do not understand the inner details of what is occurring. God will have on lookers thinking one thing when he knows the true meaning of what is happening in your life. God wants your dependency to be on him. God hears his people praying and sends people to help you out. There are times when God will not answer and your patience needs to be stretched at that point. However, he will send a new strategy in his time each. There were times, I could not see him helping me or I felt like he was not there for me, but he was helping me out of every situation. I had no idea how things would change but I knew they were changing. Each day he had me depend on him. I kept praising and praying to him and only him. My face was not down casted. My spirit believed in my heavenly father. He showed himself to me each day. He would tell me do not worry about tomorrow because tomorrow had enough cares for itself. I would be filled with living each day.. day by day. There was no secret formula but a divine intervention of his sprit dwelling on the inside of me. The assurance of faith, that cast out my doubt. My heart was heavy but my mind was fixed on Jesus.

I began to think of the story about the red sea. Moses was commissioned by God to be the deliverer of His people. He went before Pharaoh and requested the people to be let go so they may worship the Lord. Pharaoh refused and began to oppress the people of Israel even more. There were ten plagues. After the final plague, Pharaoh finally agreed to let the children of Israel go. But then he had another change of heart and chased after them with his army. "The waters were divided, and the Israelites went through the sea on dry ground, with a wall of water on their right and on their left" (Exodus 14:21–22). The "wall of water" on each side of the Israelites certainly suggests depth. Later, "the sea went back to its place. . . . The water flowed back and covered the chariots and horsemen. That's when the great scene of deliverance occurred as God parted the Red Sea. He did it for them I know he would do it for me. Exodus 14 clearly describes a supernatural event involving a deep body of water that Israel crossed on dry ground. My problems were bigger than anything I could handle …I didn't talk about them because I began to cast my cares upon the lord and he showed himself mightily in my life. He came through and he keeps coming through because I believe and trust in him and only him. There is a special protection that God has for us. He really cares and loves us. There is nothing that can separate you from his love, but your choices. As you continue to live life without him you will find yourself struggling for things to come to pass. Jesus Christ loves and cares for us and he is full of grace for his people. I have learned to go in prayer for myself. I write down my prayers according to the scriptures…. The Bible was no longer a history book but a living book of events that occurred for people just like you and me. It is my roadmap for success. Success does not come overnight but in time, God will honor his promises. This world is full calamity. We have a choice to make. Do we live for him; walking in his will and way? Or do we continue to live like the world thinking we have time to get it right?

I would always struggle and God would allow me to go into that secret place and lean on him. God has shown himself to me in so many ways… no one would ever believe it.

Questions for Study

1. Do you believe he is in control of all things?

_____
_____
_____
_____
_____

2. How often do you consult with him before making a decision?

_____
_____
_____
_____
_____

3. Are you spending your time of earthily things? How often does your decision reflect heaven?

_____
_____
_____
_____
_____

Life Application

We are the living examples. We are no longer slaves to sin but are reconciled to God. He is our father. We are both joint heirs.

Faith Response

Psalm 86:12, I will praise you, O Lord my God, with all my heart, I will glorify your name forever.

*God is my only source and
power connection*

Being equipped in the fire

How has God used you in your brokenness?

He needs to break you in order for your testimony to come out.

I was shattered but not broken. Wounded, but time has healed me.

I was placed in an environment that had consumed my ability to spend time with the lord like I use too. I love the Lord. He has always been my rock and strong tower. During this period, I was being mislead by the enemy. My mind was consumed with the day to day happenings. My thoughts were clouded and my ear was not connected to the pulse of my existence, which was Jesus Christ. I am always being lead by his spirit but that was a dark time for me. I would wallow around trying to hear from him but the cares of the job had me thinking about what I needed to do next. One day, I listened to a message and it spoke about "who are you serving?" I always thought I was serving the LORD until the minister said where do you spend your time? Where do you spend your money? What has your focus? It clicked; I had to repent and ask the lord to forgive me because my time and energy was focused on my job. I would think of the things I needed to do for work. Prior to taking that position, I would spend my time praising, worshipping, reading, writing, and talking to the Lord. My time with him was on purpose. It was never scheduled or on a time clock. I would sit still and he would communion with me about everything. I was connected to him more. My thoughts and actions were reflective of him and I was available to any and everyone. I was no longer having that experience.

I realized that my job was an idol. It had my focus. I was serving that. I was making money with this idol but this idol was consuming my time. It has taken a hold of my thoughts and energy. My mind was so focused on the next step of the enemy and time had moved so quickly. I was working underneath someone with a spirit of heaviness. This individual spent all their time on trying to be the best and a winner of being first and I believe in doing the best with Jesus instructions. I came to realize that although she spoke about Jesus I couldn't see the Jesus I had grown to know and love. The Jesus I love was open honest pure consistent never puffed up nor ready to harm anyone. The Jesus that was being portrayed was very different. I found myself needing to engage in conversations with the lord on a continuous basis because his conversations gave me clarity. I was clear in hearing myself speak and dismantled the things that clouded my judgments. My judgments were off as well as my focus. The job became a huge idol for me because it became a consuming fire. Prior to me taking the position I went there because I was told I would have flexibility in my schedule nevertheless I did not have any flexibility. I was left with responsibilities beyond my job description. The pressure was so high. I was informed that my job responsibilities included covering an entire group of people. I remember my mother saying, you are doing her job as well as your own.

I had a conversation with someone who said you went to this new position to begin the things you wanted to do for people. It was about bringing families and people together. However, I was distracted because I never got the flexibility to do what I desired. At that point I realized, I was outside of his will being mentally whipped daily by the enemy each day I would feel like a leech was sucking the blood right out of me. I could not move but when a person lives in darkness; they consume your time and their weight is transferred onto you. You need to be careful with who you let in and be prayful about your decisions and choices. However, I prayed before I took the position and I heard the lord say go.

As you wallow in self pity, you lose time on what God has called you to do and be. He never designed your life to be meaningless but meaningful for yourself and others. You are born to love. Love the person you are and the person you are becoming. He requires you to believe that you are great so rise to your greatness.

I have had so many different experiences that have created tension stress, worry, frustration, anger, and just the different levels of mixed emotions. This final position helped with my level of maturity in such a magnificent way. He showed me myself and the real love that I carry despite the things people do.

I recall God giving me an open vision. I saw myself in a fire and the fire was burning all around me, but I was walking through it. Each day has had tough circumstances but through it all. I am making it. Every day I remind myself that God is in the midst of every circumstance. My job was difficult but God gave me this promotion not because I prayed for the promotion but because he sent a word letting me know to take the job. He has continued to show me the way. I never seek him for things but ask for wisdom and strategy. I remember receiving a prophetic word from the lord; do what you will devil, but you can't stop me, you can't beat me. It is Jehovah who takes something and makes something even better. The lord is protecting me in the battle. He gave me a word and I see him moving on my behalf. I watch the faces of people or reactions when I stand up and use Gods weapons not my own. He is teaching me to engage in battle his way. My journey is not easy but his words have been spoken over me, which gives me encouragement. You need to hold on to every word that has ever been spoken over you in life. Jesus told His followers, "In this world you will have trouble. But take heart! I have overcome the world" (John 16:33). Jesus did not shy from telling His followers about the troubles they would face. It is important to remember that "our struggle is not against flesh and blood, but against . . . the powers of this dark world and against the spiritual forces of evil in the heavenly realms" (Ephesians 6:12). He has given me so many promises of things to come like having a business.

When we live our lives in disobedience to God we become unprotected. He requires us to have integrity in our thoughts and actions. He wants us to be a true reflection of him.

I remember listening to a message by Tony Evans called "Freedom from Yesterday". It was a message on forgiveness. For a person to find true forgiveness, he or she must admit the sin. This is called confession. If a person tries to pass off sin as a mere mistake, human failing, or temporary lapse of judgment; or if he or she simply denies the sin altogether, it is a barrier to forgiveness. (1 John 1:8–10): If we claim to be without sin, we deceive ourselves and the truth is not in us. If we confess our sins, he is faithful and just and will forgive us of our sins and purify us from all unrighteousness. If we claim we have not sinned, we make him out to be a liar and his word is not in us. I had to look at her as GOD see's her and forgive her for the past hurts and pains. She was only doing what someone had done to her. I said a simple pray about forgiveness not for her but for me to be healed.

The environment was so toxic and unhealthy. My peers were transferring information from her to me and me to her to keep the toxicity going but God. He began to teach me how to pray. My prayers became so specific and targeted that a co - worker said something to me when I gave her an unexpected rebuttal. She said I want a relationship with God like that. God revealed that my time with him secretly was being displayed publically. He gave me the words to say. I learned to listen to him and only him in my conversations with others. At times, I would feel frustrated. He gave me the right guidance to see my way out each time. I remember writing a scripture on my dry erase board in my office which read, "Whatever state that I am in, therefore, I will be content". I got a hold of the word and each day was viewed with a new fresh look.

She broke me down.

I felt like Daniel in the lion's den. Daniel, a law-abiding man, continued to pray to God as he has always done. Evil men, who instigated in order to entrap Daniel, they were jealous, and reported him to king. The king was forced to put Daniel into a den of lions where he would be torn to pieces. God does indeed rescue Daniel, sending His angel to shut the mouths of the lions so they do not harm him.

I am so grateful that God watches over us.

God brought me out like pure gold. There are pieces upon us that need to be refined and molded. While in the fire, he makes you moldable to withstand the test.

The Holy Spirit creates the passion of God in our hearts. You begin to see the flexibility that God has placed within you to do the things he's called you to do. I realized that my life would not have made it to this level without the different test and trials. As I was walking through them I was often discouraged believing things with my natural eyes but as I walk with the lord I see his glory in all of it. The Holy Spirit produces the purity of God in our lives. God's purpose is to purify us (Titus 2:14), and the Spirit is the agent of our sanctification (1 Corinthians 6:11; 2 Thessalonians 2:13; 1 Peter 1:2). God uses the Spirit to remove our sin from us (Psalm 66:10; Proverbs 17:3). His fire cleanses and refines. He has given me the power to handle any test burning off the things that are not like him. God moves us from level to level to level as we trust in his will and his way. There is no part of this journey that he is not aware of but an assurance of faith that moves you towards the agenda God has for you. We walk out this life wanting different things for ourselves but God plan does not always end up the same as your plan. He uses all sorts of things to remind us of his love and grace that keeps us grounded in his love and kindness. He is gracious gentle and always a present help in our time of trouble. As I think of his goodness, my heart is filled with gladness. It is truly a privilege to know I have a father that looks after me so graciously.

As you walk this journey out, you have moments of wondering if you are good enough. You are everything the father has created. Each piece of you is wonderfully made in his image and likeness. Human beings both men and women are made in God's image (Genesis 1:27; 5:1–3; 9:6; James 3:9). We did not evolve from other lower forms of life. We were created directly by God to represent Him on the earth and have dominion over every other creation in His name (Genesis 1:26–28). There is nothing he would remove or do over. You are a gift from the father precious in every way. As you begin to believe and walk in this path he has created for you. God will reveal things that are destined to flow in the way he has allowed them to shift. Your steps are ordered by the lord. The righteous are given righteousness and salvation from the Lord (Psalm 37:39). It is a psalm that reminds us of God's faithfulness, and it encourages us that we can trust Him and that He is worthy of our trust. David explains that, when we commit our way to the Lord, He will bring about our righteousness. David proclaims that God orders or directs even the individual steps of the person, and God takes delight in that person (Psalm 37:23). We do not need to create or recreate ourselves to be like others all we need to do is be who he has called you to be. The warrior is inside of you fighting to come out and take your stance. God knows you are awesome. You will have valley experiences with work, family, relationships, and personal struggles with yourself. However, trust in the lord with all your heart and lean not to your own understanding. To trust in the Lord with all our heart, we must totally rely upon God's promises, wisdom, power, and love to help us in every circumstance. Human understanding is subject to error. God, on the other hand, sees and understands all. He is the One we can lean on and trust. We should trust the Lord with all our heart because human understanding is tainted by sin, limited wisdom, impulsive assumptions, and faulty emotions. We are not always right.

Today I see his hands have been all over me. God has been walking and talking with me since I was a child. He has let me know that I am his own.

When I was young in my relationship with the Lord, people had me believe that God didn't love me because I sinned. We have all sinned and fell short of his glory but I'm so glad that he is a forgiving God not like people who look at your flaws and think they know your heart because you say nothing. Out of your heart, the mouth speaks. But we all, with unveiled face, beholding as in a mirror the glory of the Lord, are being transformed into the same image from glory to glory, just as from the Lord, the Spirit" (2 Corinthians 3:18). With those few words, "from glory to glory", Paul sums up our entire Christian life, from redemption and sanctification on earth, to our glorious eternal welcome into heaven.

Remember this:

- God's love is so strong that there is no measurement for what he will not do
- He travels from length to length to ensure that your needs are being met
- Man will try to block you but his love surpasses the distractions of others
- Keep moving in his direction not leaning on your own understanding
- His ways are never your ways

Questions for Study

1. Are you ready for God to burn things off of you?

   _____

   _____

   _____

   _____

   _____

2. Have you spent enough time with him to be equipped to walk out your journey?

   _____

   _____

   _____

   _____

   _____

3. What does your prayer life look like? Do you need to make any changes?

   _____

   _____

   _____

   _____

   _____

Life Application

You are born to love. Love the person you are and the person you are becoming. Christ will come to purify and judge. He requires you to believe that you are great so rise to your greatness.

Faith Response

Malachi 3:2, But who can endure the day of his coming? Who can stand when he appears? For he will be like a refiners fire.

Trust the process, God is doing a new
thing on the inside of you

The Lord's servant must not be quarrelsome but kind to everyone, able to teach, patiently enduring evil, correcting his opponents with gentleness. God may perhaps grant them repentance leading to a knowledge of the truth (2 Timothy 2: 24-25). God will use us in his fields, each according to our gift and the need of the moment, as we trust him.

Each day, I remind myself that no one or nothing will keep me outside of God's presence. My wall of remembrance is awesome. He has been the one and only king in my life. I recall being in a situation or at a meeting and the prophet spoke to me saying... you have the keys to the kingdom. I never understood the meaning of having keys. Keys, I thought I had special access to something or to God, but keys illustrate keeping God first. I am the key. When we keep him first in our lives he give us access to his rights, his understanding of things and we begin to make decisions based upon his will and purposes. No longer will we live by what we see, but leaning the Lord Jesus Christ. He is in control over all things. The power belongs to him and only him. Thanks be to God for taking me deeper into his word.

What a privilege to know how good he is?

The righteous are bold because they know that God is for them and what they have to say is important (Hebrews 13:6). When the apostle Paul was in prison, he wrote to the churches asking for prayer that he be bold in continuing to proclaim the gospel (Ephesians 6:19).